I dedicate this book to my loving wife Connie whose companionship at all events historical and encouragement of my endeavors in this field is unwavering. Her patience seems endless. It is also her art that embellishes this book.

I wish to thank all who made this publication possible, (alphabetically):
Mark Baker, Gerry Barker, Connie Hayes, Bob Jurgena, Karl Koster, Wayne Krefting, Rex Allen Norman, John Powers, Mark Sage, David Wright, and Shep aka "Shadow" who provided some of the photos which my wife then transferred into drawn form. Lastly my aunt, Joan Schulz, as the ruthless but loving final editor, Thank you, thank you!!

☦

"I can do all things through Christ who strengthens me."
Philippians 4:13

First Printing July 2006
Second Printing March 2021
Third Printing April 2024

ISBN 978-0-9793399-0-5 (paperback)

Copyright © 2006 by John W. Hayes

All rights reserved. No part of this publication may be reproduced distributed or transmitted in any form or by any means, including photocopying, recording or other electronic or mechanical methods without the prior written permission of the publisher. For permission requests, solicit the publisher via the address below.

Publisher:
Hunting Through History Press
38110 County Road 469
Cohasset, MN 55721
www.huntingthroughhistory.com

Printed in the United States of America

CONTENTS

Preface Page iv

1. WHAT GOOD IS A SPYGLASS IF YOU REFUSE TO FOCUS IT? Page 1.

2. WHERE HAVE ALL THE FOLLOWERS GONE? Page 25.

3. WHAT'S CREDIBILITY GOT TO DO WITH IT? Page 33.

4. A CHALLENGE MET IS A REWARD EARNED Page 41.

5. THEY'RE SO PICKY Page 59.

6. I'M NOT WEARING A COSTUME Page 71.

7. THE CONS OF ISOLATION Page 77.

CONCLUSION Page 85.

END NOTES Page 89.

APPENDIX Page I.

Preface

The main object behind this publication is to provoke thought in the hobby of recreating and portraying history in its many and varied venues. The issues dealt with in the following pages are not based on any scientifically constructed model. My own experiences were earned after a great deal of trial and error. Also, I have taken a great deal of time to speak with others around the country in an effort to get a broader understanding of the living history experience; and to compile the bits of wisdom which were so generously given to me. I am relying on the knowledge of others based upon their first hand experience and interpretation of events. In so doing I learned that a general trend is occurring across the North American continent, namely participation at Living History venues is growing. The increased participation is changing the face of "Skinner Camps" or "Ron-D-Voos" so much so that these same terms are becoming hard and fast synonyms for poor quality or dog & pony shows. The atmosphere of those camps (Ron-D-Voos) has been simply the camp should "reflect the festive spirit of pre-1840's." However, the living history venues, especially at historical sites, offer the participant more than just reflection of that festive spirit, they offer a more dependable structure based upon documented history, and a plausible interpretation of it. The Ron-D-Voo syndrome of the 1980's and 1990's still plagues a number of camps. It is not just a creature of the more loosely run Skinner Camps and Ron-D-Voos; it is a mentality born of convenience and lack of knowledge, that can still seep into and infect even well run camps.

The observations made and spoken about are based upon the experience of the speakers, your's truly included. I have six years as a board member of a living history site as well as nine years of running at least five separate specialty events (such as trade gun and woods/trail walks). I have started and run, successfully, at least two separate camps at different times of the year and helped several clubs with their shooting ranges and various competitions. I have run the trade gun competitions at several national primitive rendezvous.' I have been present at and participated in events from the North Dakota/Montana boarder to the southern tip of Illinois to southern Virginia to Northern New York. I have been in this hobby for over Twenty-three years and now it is my desire to benefit the field of living history by compiling a number of "rules," "consequences," "issues," "resolutions," and just plain "statements of fact" which will help any organizer (or participant) take an inventory of their event(or themselves). The reader will also notice that the chapters all dovetail to other chapters. The common threads that run in between all of the chapters show any reader the interconnectedness of rules, social norms, psychology, tradition, and participation not just in the living history arena, but in organizations in general, even business. I hope this publication provokes

thought, sparks conversation and leads to constructive debate. Perhaps it will cause some folks to experiment at their event in an effort to make better/tighter camps, improve the presentation at historic sites, and benefit organizations. Here's to everyone who makes this hobby work.
May God bless you in all your endeavors.

1.
WHAT GOOD IS A SPYGLASS IF YOU REFUSE TO FOCUS IT?
or
What Is My Focus?

      I have been to numerous events over the last 23 years. I attend an average of about 6 to 10 per year, approximately 10% in-door and 90% out-door. And I have to say after attending so many events and seeing the various set-ups that I appreciate a well thought out camp or trading set up. I have also seen a number of poor camps and poor events. They were poor because the organizers did not know what it was they themselves were trying to portray. Some were set up as a catch-all and others were so focused on money that they thought nothing else mattered.

      The illustration of the analogy as stated in the title is as follows: What good would it do to have a spyglass at my side if I never used it, or worse yet, every time I used it, I refused to focus it and in so doing never saw clearly the object of my attention? The sharply focused image, however, would allow me to delineate borders, determine shape and size, as well as compare and contrast shades of color. The object of my attention is my destination; therefore, I know what I am looking for because I have seen it and I can define it! It may seem like a lot of flowery talk; but, I want you to fix the picture in your mind from here on out.

I have been asked numerous times by participants and had numerous discussions with organizers of living history and rendezvous as to how to make an event work or attract a certain crowd or simply keep people coming back so that the participation does not wane. In creating an event you are giving birth to an entity which, like a child, must be nurtured, but at the same time tempered by discipline. I do not mean discipline in the sense of punishment but rather in the sense of guidance; you have to address conflicts when they arise and before they have had a chance to get too big and out of control. It means working through solutions which will allow the event to grow in a positive direction by constantly going back to the question of "What is our focus?" Growth does not necessarily mean getting bigger, it means getting better. For more on this discussion see the chapter "But They're So Picky."

As to the question of how to make an event work or turn around, my first rule of creating an event, setting up a site or staging a competition (hereinafter all collectively referred to as "event") is to ask three basic questions:

- What is my **focus**?

I determine this by making an intersect with the reference to era (period of time) and geography (physical place on the continent). I shall borrow an image of the modern scope on a rifle which has cross hairs. The horizontal line is my time and the vertical line is my geography.

- What is my **design?**

Determining design of the event is the next step. It can be determined according to the focus by asking whether the event is a large area on the frontier, at a fort, on a village path, in a city, along a street? What would have commonly existed for buildings, shelter, games, transportation, clothing, commerce, and so on?

- What **rules and policies** do I want to enforce?

Implementing the **design according to the focus** effectively and consistently is the third step. What do I want to police and enforce?

Only after I have my design in place will I be ready to make and implement the rules and policy which will do the work of keeping my event as true to history as possible.

The practical application of **focus** would be something like this: The event is the Western Great Lakes of the time period 1784 to 1820, or perhaps a more narrow, era such as the southeastern Ohio River country from 1790 to 1810 or an even more narrow to the point of staying within one year, such as 1827 at Fort Snelling. So by focusing on time and place, I have a goal, a vision, and a purpose. The words of the Bible speak directly to this point in reference to the subject of discipline, which is: But for lack of vision the people shall perish, but he that keepeth the law, happy is he. <u>Proverbs 29, Verse 18.</u> You might want to consider just how old those words are and just how applicable they still are for us today.

The practical application of **design** might require the actual building of a stockade, snake fence, piece-en-piece building, open faced shelters, as well as hiding spigots with a well house or well box, perhaps to have a tavern, a bread oven and so on.

The practical application of **creating rules**

and policies will be to look at the most plausible way of interpreting the site based upon one's present base of knowledge and how it is presently interpreted.
At that point I can prohibit certain items based upon lack of evidence in journals, or ledgers etc., but I can especially encourage the use of other items based upon those same documentary sources, and museum specimens. Give everyone a clear, concise list of the rules. That means drawing lines and making distinctions so that no one can plead ignorance of the rules. When someone crosses the line, notify them of their infraction and stand your ground. Allow them to cure or fix the problem first. If they do not comply then further enforce the rule by making the participant put away the offending item(s). If they refuse to follow the rules kick them out of the event! Remember, there may be ninety-eight others who are counting on me to hold up my end of the bargain to have a certain period camp, to enforce the rules against two others, and if grow lax I will lose the trust of the ninety-eight. In any other setting it would not be allowed that two percent of the people in the event be allowed to ignore and avoid the rules with no consequences and thereby ruin it for the ninety-eight percent. One does not have to be a tyrant but one does have to have a spine.

This brings me to the next point which struck me while talking with noted historical, author, and current staff writer for Muzzleloader Magazine, Rex Allen Norman, who asked the question:

> "Why are you doing it?? The words **re**creation and **rec**reation are spelled the same way, but simply have different inflection based upon your intent. We all do this for different reasons. The distinctions can be perceived as making lines and it makes people nervous and they don't know what to expect. The reality is that there are plenty of events for everyone."

One can say a RE-creation of history with the intent to bring alive a portion of history; versus REC-reation is like a day at the beach with the floaty tubes and cooler full of luncheon meats and soda. If the event is simply a camp where people come to participate in glorified car-camping, have a few beers, and walk around in modern street clothes, that is fine, but do not call it a pre-1840's rendezvous, it is not even historical and do not advertise it as such. There are distinctions between an historically accurate event and a simple festive setting. Be cognizant of the differences and let people know what to expect.

Furthermore if the problem with a club or event is that there are differing views which have turned into an all-out battle for several years between the "purists" and the "casual-skinners," then perhaps both sides should take a good look at what each wants. As Mr. Norman further pointed out, the "purist" side may have to say,

> "Instead of changing someone else's event, perhaps we should start a new one. That would mean a much smaller event at a different time with tighter rules and a new constituency. That would mean a new camp in which the organizers stick to the rules AT THE BEGINNING. Make new, stricter standards for a small camp. You will then have to get the word out in articles and magazines with pictures, and be ready to keep it tight."

The "casual-skinners" side can then have their same camp with its more relaxed rules; it will be smaller, but they cannot expect to attract the more serious enthusiasts. They will not have to worry about a treker's camp, flint lock prizes, hiding their beer and pop cans, or putting up with old songs and sea chanties. These people can continue to run their camps replete with bib-overalls, tackle boxes, hiking boots, and blue plastic tarpaulins as well as boom boxes, flashlights and Coleman Stoves®. If that is what they really want then, by all means let them do it.

When I spoke with living historian, interpreter and owner/manager of Frontier Resources, Gerry Barker he brought up several points which organizers should keep in mind that are illustrated as follows:

> "If I stood in the shoes of these organizations I would be looking for some objective feedback. These organizations do a disservice to other more serious historical camps when they pretend to be an historical camp, and advertise themselves as such but then have no intention of portraying history. The questions that remain for some of these people (i.e. the relaxed side) are "Who is your audience? Do we appear as a flea market full of drunks? What is our mission statement? What is our real purpose."

These are all relevant questions which unfortunately never get answered or for that matter never get asked. Another point to make is, it is a lot of work to go to a pre-1840's rendezvous, ostensibly to relive history, only to bring a whole bunch of gear to camp, most of which never gets used. Let's see, you set up the one pole tent slightly larger than the Taj-Mahal, dig the fire pit, haul out the 50 lbs. of iron ware for the fire, lug the five plunder boxes of clothes and dishes and cooking/eating utensils and the three or four coolers of beer, pop, fruit salad, cheese balls, salad dressings etc. all of which are packed into a trailer which you had to purchase and license just to carry all that gear so you could go relive history for two days and two nights...whew! That is a whole lot of work to go through just to get it wrong. So I ask, "Why go to all that work if the camp and its depiction is not even close to an historical interpretation?"

One of the reasons for this and the other essays, is to point out that Living History is growing. The number of tight, juried camps is increasing. However, I have seen the track record of the local club rendezvous' over the last 8-9 years in a number of states. I see them dropping like flies due to waning club membership and waning attendance of participants at the events. Rather than look at the way in which the event is run, these organizations try to fix the problem of waning numbers by awarding a greater quantity of prizes and more expensive prizes. My reply to this reaction is that it does no good to offer prizes to attempt to lure people into the event who have no interest in even visiting the camp, much less participating. An Organization may have the most coveted of prizes, but it will not bring in or bring back (to that loose event), the serious historical participant. The result is that no greater number of people are attracted now than were attracted before. Furthermore, I can say that after going to a number of sites that were absolutely enchanting, I felt blessed to have camped at a particular site. Then again, sadly, I knew that I would not be back because the camp was loosely run at best. I met other dedicated historical participants who felt the same way. So my observation is that no matter how beautiful the site is, if the managers or organization do not run a tight historically-based camp, then it will not bring back the serious participant. The fall-out of all that is further explored in the Essay "Where Have All the Followers Gone?"

Once again, let's go back to the focus idea. One of the glaring problems with the generic Pre-1840's event is that there are usually no parameters of time and geography; one could see a 16th century Spanish conquistador along with a 17th century Russian fur trader, along with an 18th century Tlinget fisherman as well as a 19th century Norwegian farmer; in other words a complete lack of focus. This lack of boundaries becomes a problem of having too many decades represented. However, it is easier to identify a small range like 1820 to 1840 Rocky Mountains. As for the Geography, some may say North America, but if you will notice all the origins as mentioned above could still exist. Even 1700 to 1850 is too long of a stretch for any camp. The problem with the long stretch is that people's concepts of what is possible changes.

Wayne Krefting is a long time friend of mine, a seasoned historical interpreter and the author of a recently published work on the origins and history of the pencil. Wayne had this to say, about the over-use of long time spans at events,

> "People of an earlier time could not even conceive of what was to come 50 or 100 years later. When the spread of time at an event is too large, then the atmosphere is diluted by too wide a concept as to the every day lives of the people of that time. For instance the space age of 1968 back to 150 years earlier of 1818 when steam boats were still made of wood or 1856 when only the well to do had mechanical reproducers versus 2006 when people can store 200 pictures in a chip the size of a quarter."

If the events that you attend are as loosely defined as this, where there is no "start time" but anything prior to 1840 is fair game and geography is not even mentioned, then do not be surprised to see intermingling of musketeers of the 1600's with Scottish clans of the 1300's. As you can see, it really does become a problem to police the event effectively. On the other hand, when everyone is looking at the same goal, there is a better chance for the event to continue on because the people who are attracted to it will be the audience who will appreciate it and continue to attract the newcomer with a similar vision that is needed to keep the event going.

I also had a chance to speak with several other well known historians about their view of the viability of any given event. Mark Baker, a noted primitive camper, historical interpreter and author of the countless articles for Muzzleloader Magazine, as well as the book "Sons of Trackless Forest" had this to say about events:

> "It is true to a certain extent that some events will have a life cycle in which they grow, peak then wane and even die. The exception to this phenomenon is whether the group is willing to change to adjust for new trends. If there is no inclination to change then it will fizzle. These clubs have to ask themselves, What is at the core of the event? Is it good shooting? Good trading? Good recreated fort atmosphere? More to the point, What would bring people 8-12 hours from home? I doubt that very many

would drive that far for a vaguely outlined pre-1840's event. Even the name "Rendezvous" will turn off quite a number of folks. Really when you think about it, they [pre-1840's events] are impossible to police. In my travels I am inspired by proper music from the 18th century, not amplified, along with food preparation of the period where it is cooked in bread ovens, or a pit roasted pig, calf or goat (in place of a deer). The camp games being made up of races and relays that everyone can watch, same goes for the shooting competition. When people get bored during a rainy section of weather or say... at night, they rummage through their gear and pull out and play 18th century games.

The other thing about this past-time is that when people are not paid staff they can only do so much and when they get tired then that portion of the event loses its spirit and drive and at that point the serious participants choose to go elsewhere or simply go trekking. When the original people with all the push, leave then what follows is that the people who take over may not or do not have the same push and the event wanes. ...If the people in the organization don't have the vision [anymore] then scratch it and start a new one"

I also found concurrence of opinion in the words of H. David Wright, the venerated historical artist and long time living history participant. His participation in historical events has spanned more than three decades which gives him a lot of experience. I had several conversations with Mr. Wright in which he got right to the heart of the matter:

> "Events have a life of their own and the people who started them are not the people who end up with them. When the followers do not have the same vision and drive then the event falters..... There are still a number of events which are pre-1840's events and allow anything to go on or be sold. And the public, in general, ends up seeing what they think is the way that the frontiersmen looked; with big fur hats, and lots of buckskin and knee-high boots from the '60s, and living in tipi's etc."

I mean to say that we all grew up with the frontier types on T.V. and such and we got a vision or an image stuck in our heads that it's hard to get out. I'm not saying that I don't look back with fondness on those old days because I can still remember how I felt when I would watch Fess Parker and I would want to dress up and do what he did. And that's OK because that provided a spark and that's all it took for a lot of us who watched that sort of thing..... We've all grown a little older and wiser and know that the costumes Disney used, were not what they wore back then [in the 18th century]. I'm still struggling to show people the "real thing," well we [juried participants] are all struggling... but if we give up on trying to educate the public then we're just giving in to that ole' false stereotype that seems to constantly plague us, *chuckles.* "

As an example, my abilities as an artist depend on my ability to improve and that is dependant on my acquisition of knowledge. That's the way we all learn. My paintings occurred within the full scope of knowledge at the time. Some things I painted at the time I look at now and think maybe I should not have painted that. Well, hopefully all participants grow and change as time goes on and just as hopefully the growth centers around the gaining of knowledge. There's tons of knowledge and material out there; a lot more today than there was 20 years ago and so there is no excuse to have non-period items show up in camp. There is always going to be the majority of the group who seems to go the easiest path. We should, on the other hand, strive to put that knowledge and new information to the test and the people with the drive will continue to keep a tight camp or if not, give up all together or.... go to much smaller groups."

The concerns voiced by Mr. Wright are not limited to just pre-1840 events. The plague of non-period accouterments, music and clothing can seep into any camp whether it be in the East or the West. Those of us who attend juried events should be the most vigilant in our attention to detail.

A partial list of other things that show up includes: blue speckled enamel ware, one-pole tents, baker tents, whelen tents, calicoes with more than two colors, white trappers wearing poofy coyote fur hats replete with legs and faces, aluminum ware, cheap department store moccasins sewn with shoe lace, coal oil lamps, zippers, Dyer mocs, rendezvous chairs, tackle boxes, and big commercial bowies, just to name a few. The typical rendezvous participant is not only convinced that these items existed but that they were commonly contained in a pre-1840's camp. These items should not even be seen at an event that is truly a pre-1840's event, there is way too much of this sort of thing. These items and others do not magically sprout legs and suddenly appear. Rather, they keep showing up because of the attitudes of the participants and the organizers. These people have not done or refuse to do their homework; they are still stuck in the 1980's frame of mind, *anything goes Ron-D-Voo syndrome*. That attitude is dying in some venues, but it is still prevalent enough to affect numerous other venues. The problem arises as the organizers attempt to start or resurrect an event by increasing the span of time and relaxing the rules of participation which in turn exacerbates the *anything goes* mentality. That mentality does not work at historical sites and cannot be allowed to seep into juried and other tightly run events. If it is allowed to gain a foot-hold, the event takes on an atmosphere of "what is acceptable at the last camp is ok here;" which may have **nothing** to do with history.

      To avoid falling into the *Ron-D-Voo syndrome;* our interpretation should be based upon historical information. For instance, the one-pole tent crept onto the Ron-D-Voo scene about twelve years ago. To my knowledge it is not a tent used prior to 1840 but it became acceptable because it was made of canvas and easy to erect. What should been have used all along are the wedge tents, marquis tents, Sargent's tents, and open faced shelters. Rather than play and sing a 1930's Bluegrass song, take some time to learn a few old songs from the eighteenth century or early nineteenth century. If you have a speckled enamel coffee pot leave it at home and use or borrow a tin bucket, or tin-lined copper (or brass) pot.

I had the opportunity this April of 2006 to speak with Karl Koster about running historical events. Karl is a park ranger/interpreter with the Department of the Interior at Grand Portage National Monument, Minnesota, whose duties include Bourgeois at the annual rendezvous. Karl has also started, run and assisted others in running events at several sites in Wisconsin. He had this to say:

> "When you start an event, you start as tight as possible because if you do not, it is a pain in the ---- to turn it around. If it is "Local Bob on the Back 40" and put on by the local buckskinner club it is probably not going to reach too many people. But if it is a historical site or done as a historical encampment, then you have a reputation to up-keep. If you do not then you lose credibility. When you want to

attract serious living history participants then you have to start off tight, and if you do not start off tight then you will have a reputation for being loose that will stick to you like glue and that glue is hard to wash off! The rule of thumb is: **good events breed good re-enactors**. The worst problem with old events is spineless coordinators who refuse to draw the line and commit to a position. You have to be willing to tell people their stuff is not right especially if you want the event to mature into better and better interpretations of history, clothing, social stuff, tools....

The other thing is to be cognizant of other events going on that might draw away from your event or cause conflict with the same audience that you are trying to attract."

After listening to the words of these various people and examining my own experiences, I can see that there are common threads of insight. What these contributors have said is worthy of a great deal of rumination. The salient points that run through their collective wisdom are as follows:

1) Events need to adjust/grow/change to recreate an accurate camp atmosphere that is

assembled using the present base of historical knowledge.

2) Each participant should struggle to refine and accurately portray a character in a given time period.

3) When participants and organizers do not care to use historical information to create and maintain a tight camp, then the event becomes grounded in the *anything goes Ron-D-Voo syndrome* and the serious participants will essentially go elsewhere. When the organizers do care, then the event remains historically grounded and attracts the serious historical participant and participation remains constant.

4) The event that loses its focus and dedication to history also loses spirit, drive and allows non-period things to seep into the event, gains a bad reputation and is apt to falter and begin the long descent into shrinking participation; but when the focus is kept on history, then the participants dedicate themselves to good portrayals and the reputation remains good. The result is, the participants want to keep coming back.

We (seasoned participants) have all seen events in the around the United States that operate independently of each other. Gerry Barker and David Wright have attended events in the East and South that I have not. Rex Allen Norman has attended events in the West that Karl Koster, Wayne Krefting and Mark Baker have not attended and there are events in the North that I have attended that none of these people have attended much less heard of; nonetheless, the trends are still the same and growing. Do you see a pattern at work here? Think about it. There are hundreds of events all over the United States and Canada which are not connected to each other, and yet the same dynamics are at work in most if not all of those venues.

An event benefits from participants' willingness to exhibit what they have learned about historically (and geographically) accurate clothing, games, music, skills, tools and tasks. The whole of the event benefits from the display of these things because the participants and onlookers alike encounter the surrounding portrayal of history with their five senses! Thus, does not that event become the proper place to encounter the accurate clothing, games, music, skills, tools and tasks? If your intended historical event is not doing all it can do to achieve this same result then you need to ask **why not?** Then seek the answers.

So, I come full circle to ask you again, what is your **focus**? If you do not know then you had better stop in your tracks and figure it out before you become frustrated and disillusioned. If you feel that a certain time period and geographical area intrigue you and your compatriots, then perhaps a similar audience will be lured to your event with the expectation of that **design**. You might do well to go to those venues that host your particular time and place and participate in them. Drink in the atmosphere, savor the feeling, take copious notes on that design. Then when it becomes your turn to host an event, you will have a bench mark, an identifiable goal and your market. Thus, you will create the venue for further participation by people who have the attitude for which you have been searching. Just make sure to provide guidance for your participants, which includes **making and enforcing the rules and policy** for benefit of the very people who attend.

*Author's Note- this publication went to press just after another article was published by Rex Allen Norman and though neither of us has been to the same camp, as far as we both know, his article nonetheless corresponds with this publication as I was seeing the same trends that he was also noticing. He began that article in 2002 and I began compiling the information for this publication in 2003. I direct you to A Few Good Heresies or The Trouble With Rendezvous, Rex Allen Norman, p. 33 Muzzleloader Vol XXXIII, No. 2 , May/June 2006.

2.
WHERE HAVE ALL THE FOLLOWERS GONE?

Where have all the followers gone? Hmm....sounds like it could be a hit song. On second thought, forget it. I am talking about my observations as well as the observations of other living history participants over the last ten to twelve years. We have watched numerous local rendezvous, shoots, and the clubs that support them wither and die while those curious lookers-on are busy rubbing their lower lip and mumbling, "What happened?" The answer as nearly as we have been able to determine is that these clubs for the most part were not interested in a decent historical portrayal or flat-out refused to adapt and develop into a higher level of scrutiny towards their own portrayal of history. There are many of us who, for instance, started out as generic, lackadaisical pre-1840 participants wearing fur hats and acting like the "Waaaah mountain man" we had seen on the silver screen, but something happened along the way. We began to ask ourselves, and others, "Just what did they use, wear, eat, drink or shoot, prior to 1840?" Then we started to ask others in the hobby questions such as, "Is that a period item? Is that a period style of jacket? Where can I get a good period pattern?" and so on.

Some of us became quite serious about this approach. We were having fun getting closer to recreating history, but not everyone in the club or shoot was taking it as seriously as we were. Soon different levels of authenticity were readily apparent to us. It started to become an "us and them" situation not by design, but because we wanted to do more than just pursue glorified car-camping. The "thems" began to call us names like "purist" and "Mr./Mrs. Period correct" and although it was hurled at us as a jibe or murmured towards us under the breath as a cutting insult, we shrugged it off.

What was relevant to us began to change. What caught our eye were historically oriented periodicals and the advertisements in them which listed other camps in different states. These camps were run by those who were interested in history and determined to recreate an historic atmosphere of pre-1840 or 1827 or 1792 and so on. Suddenly the thought of driving 10, 12 or 15 hours to go to a "good camp" was not so bad.

At this same time the younger participants who came to the rendezvous camps were also drawn by the idea of historical **immersion** (that was the new term of the late 1980s and early1990's) in the atmosphere of a frontier camp, fort, post or village. These neophytes came with many questions, a hunger for information, and a real desire to use their time effectively, not as another excuse to drink the weekend away.

They, more than any prior generation, saw their time as being valuable and were determined to learn about the history of their choice, be it 1600's, 1700's, or 1800's. These neophytes came to the camps for several years and during that time they slowly gravitated towards those participants who were more serious about good historical interpretation.

These hungry newcomers quickly made sweeping transformations in their dress, accouterments and attitude (including getting **rid of** the "if they would've had it, they would've used it" thought process). We older, experienced campers, who had taken fifteen to twenty years to progress to our present level, observed the newcomers make as much if not more progress than we had in a mere four to five years.

One of the reasons for the drastic difference was and is the increasing amount of historical source material in publication. What we witnessed and are still witnessing now is the trend to achieve as accurate a portrayal as possible. It is a philosophical revolution in which the people attending historical events desire to move up from the one plateau to the next. Each new level becomes an historical refinement of the previous one. The next plateau is an identifiable goal. The participant deems it worth spending his time and money on the attainment of that next goal.

In an effort to attain their goals, these newcomers had been faithfully attending the local club "Ron-D-Voos" for about three or four years. Now just at a time when a number of faltering and shrinking local clubs were looking to these newcomers as the new blood, they no longer showed up at the local Ron-D-Voos.

These same newcomers seemed to disappear off the map. They had become disappointed in having used up a whole weekend at an event wherein half of the participants really did not care about accurately portraying our historical ancestors; many of them went elsewhere and some just flat-out quit. The newcomer (who now had four to five years of experience) had seen too many shooters using tackle boxes, wearing bib overalls, walking around in biker boots with machine sewn bright orange buck-tan cowhide, in short too many "loose interpretations" and too much apathy. The neophytes had heard too many 1930's bluegrass songs, and too many modern country songs. Few if any of the old campers had even heard of, much less knew, any old songs from 1805 or 1775.

These newcomers...this promising pool of young blood...this regiment of hopefuls...went elsewhere. They no longer felt compelled to stick around to follow in the footsteps of the older members of camp. Instead, what they had found elsewhere, were a number of much smaller groups of people called trekkers who would go into the forests or primitive areas and live simply with a minimum of gear.

These trekking groups were self policing as to the authenticity of each individual; hence, each person was accountable for him or herself while on the trail or in a camp. These small groups were small enough to put on impromptu hunts, camps, and events without all of the political and bureaucratic headaches of the larger clubs and organizations.

The newcomers also found other organizers and associations committed to recreating colonial villages, military regiments, and historic battles. These organizations and venues were actually growing little by little every year.

Suddenly there were others of a like mind who appreciated the proficient and total use of the flintlock Virginia rifle, Carolina gun and Brown Bess with decent Chamber's Locks® and Coleraine Barrels®. It was a handsewn center seam moccasin or the abundance of actual buckle shoes, the sleeved waistcoat of proper cut and look, and the unabashed use of the breechclout or knee britches, that caught their eye.

Finally the games and songs which were 160, 200, 250 years old sounded as good now as they must have sounded back then. Now it was not just pop in a can with rum, it was shrub(which may or may not have alcohol). It was not just the national brands of beer, now it was micro brewed or home brewed India Pale ale or Porter each with its distinct history and usage. Now it was no longer chocolate cupcakes from the local store but Johnny cakes cooked on the fire. Instead of chocolate bars, it was chocolate drink. It was no longer Dinty Moore® from a can but rather pumpkin stew, and wild rice and grouse cooked with wild ginger root.

As an ongoing pursuit, these neophytes and the others who are interested in history are willing to try new things. They want to understand the past by letting go of the 21st Century. In doing so, they have to be (and are) willing to leave behind the creature comforts of a "car camp."

Henry David Thorough wrote about living simply with the barest of necessities, which meant letting go of modern conveniences and enduring some inconveniences and discomforts. What do you suppose those trappers and hunters, canoe men, wagoners and farmers talked about when they assembled around the fire? They talked about the hardships common to everyone, like cold winter nights, hot summer days and bugs. They could all relate to a beautiful day in contrast to a stormy night when crossing a babbling brook versus a swollen stream whilst leading a pack train. They shared their experiences with the thought that others could learn from their wisdom. The common bond between them was the fact that they were all willing to endure hardships, that complaining was a sign of a weak and broken constitution, that they endeavored to persevere. This understanding of common experiences gave birth to mutual respect.

The common thread is that these types gravitate towards others of a like mind and like experiences; and, THAT'S what the newcomers are looking for. So the lesson becomes: If one is NOT willing to venture forth and come face to face with the challenge, then don't expect any rewards and forget about trying to understand those who do want to face those challenges.

So now I ask you, Where have all the followers gone? My answer is: They have not gone at all. They are quite alive they and can be found at well run historical camps. These camps are filled with participants who want to meet the challenge of a well run period camp.

And of the local clubs, when will they ever learn? Well, now, that is the question, isn't it? But we know that if they do not care about recreating some portion of history, then they will not learn. They will have fallen behind. They will wither and die the slow death of apathy. Simply put, there is no following someone when they have fallen behind.

For further reading see the article <u>Thinking Out of the Box, Recreating Trapper Camps: Part I</u>, Rex Allen Norman, p. 52, Muzzleloader Magazine, May/June 2002 issue.

3.
WHAT'S CREDIBILITY GOT TO DO WITH IT?

No this is not a new Tina Turner song, but rather a critical question for every manager, promoter, and board who runs an event, or an historical site. It also affects the media in its presentation of history and the idea of "Getting it right, getting it correct." It is not just the idea that something is believ-**able**, but rather the assurance that an interpretation is actually based upon sound research. This question may also be posed thusly: "What does legitimacy have to do it? Think about a middle aged woman visiting a physician and she may question whether he is a legitimate or a fly-by-night operation. When second and third opinions are received from other doctors and are congruent with the first's prognosis or diagnosis, then that first physician has gained credibility in her eyes. She feels better about placing her reliance in the information presented to her by the physician. Reliance, in the legal arena, is actually one of the factors in determining whether a plaintiff has been defrauded. Simply put, FRAUD means the person relies on a statement of truth that is actually false.

The person parts with something of value and later finds out that what he has received is NOT what he bargained for; in other words, it is broken or fake!

How about those stereotypical icons of the used car lots; those often-maligned salesmen who will do anything to make a sale and tell us what we want to hear instead of answering our questions with factual information. How many of them are trusted by the general public? Ask yourself: Is that how you want to be perceived? I should think not! Do you think, on the other hand, that the honest used car salesmen enjoy having to struggle against that stereotype just to get you to a point where you are willing to listen? Perhaps then and only then will the common person be willing to, at the very least, consider trusting what is being said. That is a whole lot of work just to deliver the common person to a point where he is willing to open his mind, ever so slightly, to believe the information given to him, which then may lead to the possibility of a sale.

In short and simple terms, when any participant in the living history circles attends an event, it must be in their minds, first of all, a legitimate use of their time and resources such as gas, and money, but also of information, networking, and new chances to spend time with people of like mind. What makes an event "Good" can be subjective. However, to say objectively that the presenters, participants, merchandise, social framework and a host of other aspects are **legitimate** is to say that the interpretation of them is

    1) from historically accurate information,
    2) enables a believable depiction, and
    3) allows reliance on a basis for a correct style and cut of clothing (or firearms or wagon or pottery). Experimenting with the same or similar tools leads one to discover the real mode of manufacture.

Experimentation with period games, with period dance steps, with period food preparation, etc., all lead to a credible or believable interpretation which is relevant to us because it is not fake! Rather, it has its roots in the actual life-skills of our ancestors. In more concrete terms, the peddler or monger in dressed in appropriate clothing for the period, using tools and accoutrements of his station, and selling goods or presenting information that can be documented to his particular time and place makes him a credible figure or persona.

    Mark Sage is an author, historian and

historical participant in numerous eighteenth century venues and has been giving lectures on the eighteenth century common hunter for well over a decade. He had this to say about fulfilling the role:

> "A serious historical <u>participant</u> needs to feel <u>he is</u> the character. I call this *skin-side-in*, meaning we are the character on the inside. We feel and react as that historical character would have acted, versus the outward appearance of merely wearing the clothing without the mind set which would be termed *skin-side-out*. The difference is; the participant works at and tries to get into the head of their character. Anyone can put on clothing, and purchase look-alike-gun, knife, hat and accoutrements and simply look the part. But to really be the part one must adopt the culture, mind-set, mannerisms and so on. Don't just put the outfit on; BE THE CHARACTER! Don't just act the part like a Hollywood extra; BECOME THE PERSONA. Let the persona become you! For instance: when at an event, instead of just being physically there; step into the character and by doing so, step into the reality of the time which you are trying to portray. Thus it means a good deal more than simply carrying a good gun and wearing a good shirt. Some of us live in the clothes

when not at work. They are worn while gardening, gathering wood or butchering while using the proper hand tools to build things fences and sheds. Again using the proper tools while wearing the clothes ensures they will become sweaty and dirty and worn. We then have the first hand knowledge of just how useful and tough or how useless and bad a given cloth, leather, hat, knife, ax or gun can be. I can remember the Mel Tillis song "You're Just a Coca-Cola Cowboy" which by changing the label you could say that someone is a Coca-Cola Frontiersman because they simply look the part. What they are missing is the background and mind-set of the part. Without knowing how the character thought and why (due to religion and culture), a participant is simply wearing a set of clothes."

In fleshing out the idea of the total person, it once again goes back to having good or first hand knowledge which shows in the participant's familiarity with something as mundane as how clothing, tools, kettles and baggage may look after a great deal of wear and tear, cooking, and travel. *(See also the chapter "I Am Not Wearing a Costume")

Further, to those of us who expect that credibility, the whole scene of a shabbily dressed street monger or a coal besmudged blacksmith plying his trade or a non-laboring gentleman wearing white stockings at a event or historical site is now a legitimate portrayal, a REAL or CORRECT thing. We want to accept that the goods for sale (and how they are interpreted) are the same or similar to those of 200 years ago for that time and geographical place. We want to rely on the presenter's knowledge. We want to trust his depiction, we want to have faith in the sales person's information and recommendation. We want to know that what we have received is not fake or broken or completely wrong.

      This also pertains to how well an event is policed according to the rules as posted, or as happens all-to-frequently, how loosely the site or event is run by those in charge. For example if the rule is: **No cigarettes - only pipes of the time period may be smoked**, then there should be absolutely no cigarettes, period! Further, those in authority should not allow any exceptions. Since we are attempting to recreate an historical venue, then logically we need to eliminate those items that are completely out of place and that detract from the scene. The participants by and large have worked hard to make sure their camp or table of goods is filled with appropriate items and have every right to expect that the rules will be followed by everyone else.

The end result is that we ask ourselves the question above in a different form: Is this a believable or credible scene? Does this camp accurately portray a certain decade and geographical location? Did the pill box for sale even exist at that time? When those events and historical places gain our favor then they become a legitimate example of a place that we would like to visit or like to recommend to our friends and acquaintances. Lastly when the event or site consistently maintains those high standards, it gains a reputation for being a credible example of time, place and manner. Therefore, as we look at the calendar we are reminded that on a particular weekend of May, June, or October a well-run event will occur at a particular site. Not only will it occur, but its presentation will be anticipated by those who enjoy it and are impressed by it. If, on the other hand, the event or site is poor in its presentation, the standards are ignored, and rules for participation are not enforced, the participants soon begin to see it as a waste of time, and the public asks whether the organization is legitimate or just another in the long list of sham theme parks whose only purpose is to suck the money out of the unsuspecting public. Again ask yourself, Which one do you want to participate in?

Therefore, if your event/site/organization is seeking participation to swell its ranks with credible and active participants and to encourage a steady flow of public or customers, you must ask the sometimes painful questions of another outside observer. That must be a person who is terribly honest and will tell you <u>*whether your presentation is credible*</u>. Does it seem to others as a valuable use of time? The answers may lead you to the goal of actually finding the legitimacy you seek.

4.
A CHALLENGE MET IS A REWARD EARNED
A response to the question,
Doesn't a beginner need to start somewhere?

The very quality that brings a beginner into living history settings is atmosphere. It should be like being transported back in time. A well run event will leave the beginner with the feeling he has hit the historical jackpot. As an organizer, promoter, or board member keep reminding yourself of the goal: I **DO** want the beginner to come back. One of the best ways to accomplish this goal is to keep your camp tight which will keep the good and serious living enthusiasts returning as well as give the beginner some substance to provoke his own thoughts of historical context.

Having said that, it is inevitable that the question will arise, "What if I make it too hard?" The complaint to support the question is as follows: *If an organization or club makes its standards too tough it will scare away the beginners.*

Yes, it may very well do that; but more importantly, the crux of the matter is to ask in return, *What sort of participants are you looking for?*

And further follow up with the question,
> "Wouldn't you rather have participants who do all they can to improve the event, rather than people who are constantly looking for ways around the rules and forcing exceptions?"

In short, do not worry about making it too hard. The alternative result is that those who are looking for an excuse to relax the standards will tout the war cry, "Well, the beginner needs to start somewhere!" This is generally said with all the plaintive whining of a youngster begging for an excuse, any excuse, not to have to work a little bit and in the process unwittingly improve himself.

The fact of the matter is, if the new participant wants it badly enough, he will attain the minimum threshold for entry into the club or event. When a goal is worth achieving then it will take some work to achieve it. Lo and behold, it will taste all the sweeter.

Any one of us is going to have to work at something in order to attain our goal. If a goal is made too easy, then there is no appreciation of it. Therefore, if you are running a good camp, do not worry about making the camp standards too tough. Camps that challenge participants to attain historical authenticity will by their very nature reward the whole of the camp with a good atmosphere and the event will continue to attract newcomers. Hence, the rule is the very statement in the title, "A challenge met is a reward earned."

This is also a good reminder for some of us old-timers in this living history venue. Just because we, as experienced participants, have been at this sport for Twenty years is no excuse to get lazy with our camp, clothes, accouterments, or set-up. The inevitable fallout will be a good deal of resentment and argumentative questions like, "How come he does not have to follow the rules?" It's a good question... and we all know the answer ......there is no excuse! So do not allow any exceptions, whether beginner or old timer.

When the rules go slack, then the event goes slack, then participants begin to question whether it is worthwhile to attend the event; suddenly there is a noticeable drop in attendance. Rather than attracting quality in a serious historical participant, the organization **unfortunately** begins to focus on pure numbers and will take any participant. In the matter of several seasons the event is now attended by an over-abundance of ...well... slobs.

Now ask yourself: Why would a beginner want to come to an "historical setting" which has been advertised as Pre-1840, but all he sees in camp are plastic orange juice jugs next to the pink styrofoam egg carton amid the mountain of beer cans, and just for good measure a couple of disposable flash lights all atop the vinyl covered aluminum table?????

Oh yeah, don't forget the plastic beads on the commercial knee-high moccasins with the foam rubber soles being worn by a person toting a plastic tackle box filled with supplies to load the stainless steel barreled rifle with the ryanite stock and day-glow peep sights. Gosh, doesn't that just stir your early American spirit? Doesn't that just bring you back to the historical times? Isn't that just so realistic? What? It doesn't do anything for you?

Perhaps a camp wherein the rules of authenticity are actually enforced might do it. Ya' think? OK, I'm getting a bit sarcastic, but you can see the point. Once you lose your legitimacy, it is hard to get it back. At that point forget about the beginners starting anywhere, because now they have it firmly fixed in their mind that your event/organization is a farce and no one is really taking this living history thing seriously at all. The potential newcomers' conclusion will be, they have just wasted their time.

Any time an organization puts on an event, it is also simultaneously advertising and marketing its efforts by connecting with other people of a like mind. So, by bringing into the fold a beginner who is enthusiastic about the living history period, which your organization is recreating, you are benefitting from that person's energy. By giving that beginner good models, that person will also want to recreate a good model in themselves.

Let's flesh out the example of a club that fails or refuses to follow tighter standards with the alleged intent being that the camp has to allow beginners to get started. This common scenario begs the question, "When does a club get to the point where it no longer is catering to just the beginner? The point is that the club which never gets past the "Beginner Stage" is simply a camp full of beginners who have been stuck in that place for 6 or 8 or 10 years. Furthermore, if beginners are not forced to seek higher levels, to attain more mature interpretations, to graduate to higher levels, (if you will) they do not develop. They do not progress. When the camp is only geared towards the beginner, then the camp as a whole does not progress. The result is that beginners are constantly allowed excuses for not attaining a level of entry.

When these exceptions are constantly made, then the exceptions become the rule and the larger rules no longer have any meaning and they simply disappear. I say it is up to the beginner to jump in and hold on. It is up to the club to run the event for the good of the **whole camp**.

As for HOW do you get started; keep in mind the KISS principle, viz., **K**eep **I**t **S**imple **S**illy. What does the beginner really need in order to get going, and more importantly, in order to progress? Certainly they do not need all the bells and whistles and as stated above the beginner can avoid costly mistakes. Buying an inappropriate pair of shoes can be costly at $150.00 to $200.00 per pair.

In speaking with the seasoned, historical interpreter John Powers, I am reminded of a well produced, conducted, and run camp put on just for beginners. There was no dress code, no historical camp standards, with the main idea being to 1) ease the anxiety level, 2) prevent the beginner from making costly mistakes, 3) give them a pool of information and experienced campers for answering their questions. The event lasted only three years, and due to lack of funds and help, it had to be dropped.

The positive aspect is there were two or three "newbies" who got the idea and hit the ground running and continue to progress in their interpretations.

The negative aspect is there were also a

number of participants who did not progress and continued to show up in their tennis shoes and Docker's® shorts all three years. I recall one individual who finally borrowed an old looking shirt, but it was still the wrong era, and he was still wearing his modern shorts and tennis shoes.

My interpretation of this experiment is that there was no follow up to see that each participant continued to move toward being an active historical participant. There was no minimum threshold to attain before being able to participate in a full fledged camp. There was no graduation process and no push to keep on progressing. Lastly, the (mental) challenge to the neophyte seemed only theoretical. There was no real test.

John Power's interpretation is this:
> "The camp did prove its worth because it kept people from making costly mistakes. It got at least 2 or 3 pointed in the right direction, and it created a mechanism for getting people involved because it really can be awkward to get involved in someone else's game."

Mr. Powers did go on to add though:
> "At Grand Portage [Minnesota], which is a good camp, well attended by good, savvy,

historical participants the general public or interested newbie is much, much more likely to come upon several quality presenters, good historical information and knowledge based upon sound research, than they would if going to a skinner camp.

I believe Mr. Powers has valid points. I give him (and Ken and Bonnie Swanson) a great deal of credit for putting forth a mountain of effort to create an event, with the laudable purpose of bringing in new blood.

Though Powers and I may differ in our interpretations on the results of the "newcomer event," we do both agree on the proposition that excellent historical camps produce excellent historical participants. We both continue to squeeze in time, in any number of camp settings, to teach the public as well as the newcomer about history AND the hobby. We are always happy to have new blood with a passion for history!

Also, we agree that one of the problems that plague the local/skinner camps is the "rendezvous syndrome." This syndrome is a culture of its own, much of which is NOT based upon history but simply what is acceptable at "Ron-D-Voos" in general. A person who attends only these camps will be given the wrong impression that, for instance, commercial or lasted moccasins were common, that hunters wore foot long fringe on their heavily beaded, leather jackets, and that any white speckled enamelware actually existed in common form, all before 1840.

    The truth is none of these things existed in those forms in that time period. If, however, a likely camp-goer does not venture to other historical settings such as re-enactments, juried events, military musters, period-treks and historical seminars then, that camp goer is missing the rest of the journey to continue to improve his own historical interpretation.

    Therefore, my advice is to treat the journey as just as much a part of the process as the destination(s). The newcomer should take some time and develop a feel for what he really wants to portray. One approach to answering this question is: What portion of history do I really want to experience or "re-live?" The answer to this question especially will prevent the newcomer from paying $1,000.00 on a tipi or giant One-Pole that he may never be able to use at any events in his chosen time period and geographical location.

    Also remember, getting started in this hobby is no different from any other; thus, "The beginner will have to start at the beginning like everyone else," and that means he or she simply needs to show up at meetings, functions, and events and confer with members and others who are in the particular club or organization. As for the hopeful living history participant, that person must acquire the basic clothing to enable him to fit in and participate in the general goings-on. Further, reading materials have never been in greater supply. There is a wealth of information in print that was not available to the common person 25 years ago.

   The situation in which a beginner feels he is not ready, may stem from a lack of confidence in his presentation (clothing, accouterments, camp etc). We older members and participants owe it to him to gently scrutinize his work and give him sound instruction for improvements. This includes reading and source material, as well as reassuring him of all the things he is doing right. But here is the real key, which is no secret: A person who has excellent models to emulate will be much more likely to be an excellent model himself and in turn be better enabled to contribute to the atmosphere of the event and the good of the organization. This dynamic has existed for thousands of years. It is, in itself, one of the cornerstones of education.

As an analogy, think of a tool and die maker who crafts an excellent mold for brass candle sticks with the end product generally being a well molded product with few if any flaws and virtually no seams to file down. The fresh casting will require a minimum of work to take off a few rough edges, buff and polish to arrive at a valuable finished product.

If the mold is, on the other hand, a poor one, the halves of which are off-center, and the brass is poor and dirty, then the product will require a lot of extra work. Someone must not only take off rough edges and fill in pock holes, but also do extra filing to smooth out the seam left by the poorly fitted molds. Even after much more buffing and polishing, perhaps it will be realized that the piece is substandard, the brass candle stick will have to be melted down, and one must start all over again. I liken this analogy to the people using hard earned money to purchase items which are inappropriate to time, geography and status.

Times are changing and more than ever people want to be able to show some value for where and how they have spent their time and money. Any experienced participant, as an objective observer, can point out a number of areas in which the neophyte is doing well and in so doing give him or her the encouragement needed to keep progressing.

People in general value correct information. The law demands it. The public is owed correct information especially when admission fees to historical venues are necessary. Therefore, after spending time and money to travel to a location, whenever I can glean a nugget or two of lore and wisdom, I feel enhanced by the scholarly efforts of others. Since I consider that particular encounter worthwhile, I also feel that my time and money have been well spent. I then gladly conclude that my trip as a whole was worthwhile.

Too, the beginner should, if possible, have a mentor or teacher, of whom they can ask a great many questions and that person can also connect the beginner with others who have particularized knowledge of clothing, mannerisms, customs, geography, accoutrements and so on. These examples are just the tip of the iceberg:

manners- Common folks have less material wealth but they are not stingy. Lack of education does not mean lack of manners in the house or around women, children, and guests.

customs- Those of lower status tip their hats to those of higher class. Those of higher class are referred to as "betters." Calling a person a coward was a serious insult.

geography- Settlers had specific routes to and between the settlements. Ethnic groups settled in certain area when arriving from Europe. Sailors had specific trade routes such as the triangle trade viz. rum, kegs/slaves, sugar cane, molasses.

eras- Time period is important when considering the fashion of clothing, usage of tools, availability of firearms, and types of water craft manufactured. For instance the button fly(on britches) was used after and during the usage of the French Fly. The sack back gowns came into usage late in the third quarter of the 18th Century. Trousers were worn by laborers in the 18th century. By the first quarter of the 19th century the younger men wore trousers and adopted pantaloons (which had been prior to that time strictly military), but the older men tended to stick with knee britches, The prairie or sun bonnet was NOT WORN until the 1850's.
By the way, the 18th century is the 1700's and the 19th century is the 1800's. If you do not believe me then just look to our own century. The 1900's is the 20th Century and the 2000's is the 21st Century. So in your reading and research be careful to note

whether the subject is the 1800's or the 18th century. There is a big difference!
At this point I would strongly suggest two books by the author, artist and naturalist Cathy Johnson;

> 1) Living History, Drawing On the Past, Johnson, Cathy, Graphics/Fine Arts Press, P.O. Box 321 Excelsior Spring MO 64024, © 1994.
>
> 2) Who Was I, Creating A Living History Persona, A modest Guide to the Hows and Whys., Johnson, Cathy, Graphics/Fine Arts Press, P.O. Box 321 Excelsior Spring MO 64024, © 1995.

As a newcomer to the living history arena, if you do nothing else for the first year or two, you should at the very least obtain one **basic** set of clothing for the era and geography in which you are most interested. This is again just the tip of the iceberg. A man can achieve the simple task of basic 18th Century style as follows:

-obtain a body shirt of white and perhaps a box frock of an earth tone color such as gray, brown, tan, golden rod, dull blue, dull burgundy and the ever present white. Remember trousers are generally worn by the working class and slaves. I said generally, as there are always exceptions.

Knee britches are very common and there are even accounts in various papers or *Gazettes* which describe indentured servants and slaves wearing knee britches.

   -Use a neck cloth of silk, fine linen, fine cotton

   -For a hat, there are many such as a banyan hat/cap (a 2023 correction in which the 4-pannel or workman's cap was removed), felt wide brim, scarf, forage cap, Canadian cap, knit cap such as a sailors or Machault cap.

   -For shoes a simple pair of shoe pacs or shoes without buckles, or moccasins will go just about anywhere in the North American Continent. Just remember, there are many variations of moccasins, each geographic area of the continent has a style(s) which are particularly suited to that particular climate, terrain and tribe. Wooden clogs for the French or Dutch farmer *may* be correct, for your portrayal.

Now on to the eating utensils:

   -one spoon to use as your own. It is as personal as your toothbrush.

   -one wooden bowl or wooden trencher (plate) to eat out of and wash as soon as you are done

   -one tin plate upon which you can put cooked food

      *Notice there is no mention of a fork. They

are generally used for cooking, but they are not used for eating among the vast majority of people. Food is generally conveyed to the mouth by use of the spoon, knife or fingers. Yes, that's right, if you want to eat a salad use your fingers!

To cook:

  -Two kettles: One 3qt and one 5qt, which if made of brass or copper be sure that it is tinned on the inside. Some are lined with nickle which is okay. In one of these you cook rice, beans, stews and soups. In the other you make coffee or heat water.

  If you get a frying pan or spider (fry-pan with three legs) then obtain a sheet metal one, not cast-iron. Cast iron is heavy and would be used in a homestead or settlement. It would take the most likely shape of a small cauldron or kettle rather than a fry-pan.

  Now, the trick is to try a few meals at home to get the hang of cooking on these simple contrivances. This will give you the confidence to use them when you arrive at camp. As with any new project, there is trial and error. My hope is that you will not only have "successful trials," but also "teaching errors." If you make a mistake, learn from it. We as adults are given the dignity to fail. Sometimes we learn more by our failures than by our successes. That's why it is called: trial AND error. Do not be afraid to ask questions and keep on **doing.** When you, as the beginner, are feeling overwhelmed just remember. "The best way to eat an elephant is **one bite at a time."** Also, keep in mind: A challenge met is a reward earned.

5.
THEY'RE SO PICKY

Rules are enacted and enforced to provide guidance. Historical events need rules and cannot be expected to run in the absence of rules. With those rules in mind we should strive to not only follow them, but find other ways in which to improve an event. We show respect for others who have worked hard to conform to the rules by doing the same ourselves. We all have choices in our lives. Even if we choose not to decide, we still have made a choice!

Each event has its own reputation for following rules and even though 95% of the participants have no trouble following the rules, it never seems to fail that the 5% who do not want to follow the rules scream the loudest about the "nit-picky" attitude of the people running the event. For those of us who have been given the appellation of "purist" we actually *like* the idea of a set of rules for authenticity being enforced. When and if a participant has a problem with the strictness of an event; he has the choice to leave, perhaps not even attend in the first place, OR attend and abide by the rules like everyone else.

For those participants who want exceptions and always tend to focus on how to get around the rules and argue for loopholes, then I say that strict or juried events are not for them. As for you organizers, those same people will make every attempt to dilute the application of the rules and try to make you, the "enforcer," look like an uptight, compulsive control freak. That might well be the case, but remember you are trying to run an event or get an event (or new site) off the ground successfully and especially *correctly!* Thus, you *should be* concerned with the details.

This same thing can affect an event that has been running for many years. Despoilers will get in and generally their bad attitude will not be apparent until later. They do not have signs on their forehead marking them as troublemakers. When trouble starts, however, you as the coordinator or manager cannot allow them to badmouth and taint your event. You need to quell them or boot them. If they are not cautioned on their behavior or removed, they will succeed in ruining the event for the other law abiding participants.

There is nothing wrong with active criticism, but it should be within the context of portraying history as accurately as we can do, given the way in which the current base of knowledge is interpreted. To do otherwise is to simply gripe, complain and destroy.

A friend of mine, Bob Jurgena, is a member of an association called the Chasseurs du Datchurat at Fort des Chartres in lower Illinois. This association is responsible for putting on an especially tight event (*see note end of chapter).

One day Bob was confronted by a particularly belligerent, potential participant to whom Bob refused admission because the newcomer did not meet the historically strict standards of the camp. Bob was told by this snarly individual that the event would never increase in numbers, to which Bob replied that his group did not care if it got bigger, because they were more concerned about it getting better. (On a side note, the event continues to grow year after year because of the fact that it is so tightly run!). Bob later related to me:

> "Our group's main concern is that it gets better and keeps getting better. This event has little to do with hundreds of people, but it has a lot to do with a high quality of interpretation."

He further added,

> "Good participation means you shouldn't

> ever have to remind them [the participants] of the rules."

Events can get bigger in two ways;

> 1) more people participating;

As an organizer if more people fit the criterion for a narrow time period then let them in.

> 2) larger spans of time used for

participation. An event allowing interpretation from 1670 up to 1850 instead of a more narrow band of participation such as 1755 to 1785, will increase numbers but may seriously dilute atmosphere.

What I have also found after starting up several events myself, as well as starting and running successful contests for well over ten years is that, as a rule, the level of scrutiny at which you begin an event will rarely ever and probably never get more strict than when you began. The caveat to that would be that if the organization or managers of the event want to tighten up they have two choices;

> 1) Institute changes to limit what is acceptable in camp or on-site during the event and do it over a several year time frame. To tighten up an event, or site, takes a long time. The process must be implemented incrementally over time, with

plenty of notice to the attendees.
2) Simply shut down the event, or let it die for a year, and then begin again under stricter controls with no one grandfathered back in; each person must be admitted upon his or her own merits.

I have been asked by a number of people at small or local events, "What can we do to attract more people?" or, "How can we stop the steady attrition in our numbers?" My answer to both questions is commonly and remains:
"You (your club, organization, group) will have to tighten up your standards and implement controls on what is acceptable and then absolutely enforce your rules and make no exceptions."

Unfortunately and all too often the response right back at me is "Well, yea, but...besides that....." I must conclude at that point, that the person did not catch what I said because he did not deem my ideas relevant or he simply felt that the concept of having to run a tighter ship does not apply to him.
I can think of no less than five local clubs that are all now defunct who all thought that very

observation did not apply to them. Either way, if they miss the point, they are not seeing the real problem. This can be stated as follows: IF it is all things to everyone then it is nothing to any one person.

For instance, to a wine connoisseur, a wine cannot be both a Merlot and a Port. To a beer connoisseur, an ale cannot be both a Porter and an India Pale Ale. To the cook, a burger cannot be both 100% beef and be 50% turkey. To the outdoorsman, a water craft cannot be both a canoe and a run-about. To the gun enthusiast, a rifle cannot be both a lever action and a fully automatic sub-machine gun. Hopefully you, the reader, can see a pattern.

The element of choice is the key. You must choose what you want your camp to represent. Pursuit of a goal cannot be successful unless the object of that pursuit is first defined. If you the promoter want your event or site to represent a fur post then you must make the decision to narrow it to a certain time i.e. 1790 to 1802 as well as make the decision what geographical location you want your camp to represent i.e. Yellow River in the Northwest Territory (Wisconsin). Perhaps in an effort to tighten up your event you want to narrow the camp to 1790 to 1814 in the Red River Valley of the North, instead of the generic pre-1840 without geographical parameters; that choice is up to you. If you choose to do nothing and your event continues to decline, because it is too loose, then do not expect any changes. The unspoken rule in trying to effect change is: *If nothing is different, nothing is different.* It may sound redundant but think about it. If what you are doing is not working, then you need to change something. If you do not do so, then the very thing that is not working will continue not to work.

  Therefore, if an event is strictly a French and Indian War period event, then any person or business that displays accoutrements or items from 1770's era should not be allowed to participate. Likewise, if an event is 1784 to 1820, then the oil lamps from the civil war period do not belong there, should not be sold, used or even seen. If an event is the year of 1827, then the Colt Patterson pistol does not belong there, should not be sold, used or even seen. If an event is pre-1890, then little pictures of Mount Rushmore, modern glass dragons, and 1950's resin composite dolls do not belong there, should not be sold, used or even seen.

  I have witnessed the following: When the managers, promoters, and organizations are faced with the participants telling them that the event is too loose and needs to tighten up, what the participant means generally is that the rules for the time period are not being followed, i.e. 1750 to 1798.

What the event organizers end up doing is simply allow the event to host a larger time span i.e. 1680 to 1870 which in the promoter's mind he thinks will cure the problem of the non-conforming items or camps or tables. This is the very mistake that takes a specific event and turns it into the proverbial "everything to everyone."

The other consequence from this sort of reaction is that the organizers have now just compounded their policing problems many times over because now there is the need for knowledgeable persons and experts for all of the additional decades that have been added. The problem has not been solved; rather, it becomes harder to hold the organizers accountable for a "loose camp" or non-conforming merchandise.

This is not to say that <u>time line</u> events are loose affairs. On the contrary, I have conferred with organizers and attendees of those events and have been told that there are committees (of one or more persons) for certain eras, decades, and specific battles or settlements. Thus, a person or committee is now accountable for policing that particular part of the event with all the pickiness of other camps in far away places.

The last point to be made about the tightness or strictness of a camp that should be clear to all in attendance is the **Starting and Ending times** for a given Event. These times should, for instance, run from some time Friday night (like 12:00 a.m. midnight) to the following Sunday afternoon, say at 4:00 p.m. Every participant must be properly attired and accoutered during that time while on site.

To maintain authenticity for a mere 40 hours is not that onerous. The average person can do without all of the creature comforts for that short a time.

However, strictness is not a sledge hammer to be used to swat a mosquito. At any number of juried events, participants are staying in tents made of vivtex® or sunforger®. Further, in most of these contexts (other than strict experimental studies, and period craft fairs) whether the wool is 100% or 85/15 makes little difference, just as machine versus hand sewn is not always readily apparent. Whether the spindles on a chair or wheel are hand turned or machine turned rarely affects the caliber of the interpretation. But believe you me, those of us who have been labeled as purists definitely appreciate the difference in the attention to detail.

If you the reader are still skeptical, let us delve into another appropriate example.

How would you feel if you had struggled and slaved to attain an acceptable level of authenticity for a given camp, but when you wake up Saturday morning your neighbor is still wearing blue jeans and a Hawaiian shirt? He has a gas stove on a modern folding table from a discount store, with a couple of empty Pringles® Potato Chip cans and a half-full bottle of spiced rum in its commercial plastic bottle. Worse yet, these things remain out in the open until about 2:00 p.m. Saturday afternoon. My first question would be "How did he get in?" Sadly, and more to the point, "What am I doing here?"

Keep in mind that the organizers are trying their best to make the event conform to a certain *time and place*. Their pickiness also shows that they care about the atmosphere, legitimacy, and success of their event. So, the next time you read rules that prohibit modern glasses, modern 20th and 21st century pipes, cigarettes, modern jewelry, plastic, nylon, aluminum, etc., respect the rules or do not attend. Also, guess what...a juried or tightly run event is bound to have a number of learned historians, collectors, writers, curators, and primitivists; in other words, there is a well spring of historical knowledge and a pool of personel who do not mind answering questions. My gosh! Think of it. These learned people usually love to talk about what they do.

    If you think you are ready to attend a well run, strict or juried camp then put yourself to the test. See how well you, yourself, stack up. Those strict organizers are putting on a strict event for the benefit of the participants, they are not doing it to make you angry or to pick on you. They are placing their neck on the chopping block of accountability. So before you say, "They're so picky," ask yourself, "Could **I** do as well?"

*Chapter note, La Compagnie des Chasseurs du Datchurat, no longer run the Spring Trade Faire at Ft. des Chartres, but turned it over in 2018 to Les Amis du Ft. des Chartres, who continue to carry on the juried event.

Robert Jurgena passed away in 2022, he contributed much.

6.
I AM NOT WEARING A COSTUME

The question has been asked of me a thousand times, "Where did you get your costume?" I politely reply that what I am wearing are real clothes with real sweat, grease, blood, dirt, food stains, and patches.

"Costume" conjures up images of halloween and of clothing that is a mere facade, a substitute, a romantic *looking* image of earlier garments. It also is applied to the term for fake jewelry, viz "costume jewelry."

I flinch every time I study a pamphlet that reads "...costumed interpreters..." My thought is that if a person is interpreting history such as George Washington's crossing of the Delaware, or a character such as Daniel Morgan, "The Old Wagoner," or a common person making Windsor chairs, chances are he will not have gotten his clothing from the local costume shop. He instead will be wearing a fashion of the "cut and cloth" that is common to that era and geography, station, status and so on. If that interpreter or juried participant has not made it himself, he probably purchased it from someone who did know how to make it, a reputable seamstress.

To call it a costume is to imply that the

interpreter is doing nothing more than creating a fantasy such as Superman, Mickey Mouse, Cinderella, or Spider man, an image on paper, something and someone displaying powers and abilities that never existed in reality.

 The other facet about costume that is not immediately seen, felt or even smelled is that of actual wear and tear. In case you have never stopped and thought about it before, everyday clothing gets used and worn, which means they become thread-bear in the wear spots. Buttons fall off after significant wear. But just as importantly, they soak up all the smells of a cooking fire, a horse, a cow, an arm pit, just as they will soak up spilt wine, beer, dye, grease, and silt.

 Given the sensitivities of people now-a-days, however, we can only wear clothes so long before we cannot stand our own smell much less the smell of others. The military types refer to this as "funk," and everyone who is out in the bush for a week or more with no shower develops a smell and the clothing picks up that smell. It is one thing when all your comrades have it along with you, but if you stand out in the crowd because your socks and pantaloons also stand up in the crowd without you in them, then the general public will be distracted by the "parfume."

 Except for strictly interpreted settings, we do not have to go that far, but do keep in mind that a good many people in the first three quarters of the 18th Century may have washed only several times per year and that was in the warm months.

We as interpreters who are involved in experimental archeology and who also show up at events with our well worn clothing can comment first hand as to the durability and usefulness of practical clothing.

When the public sees us as common folks, they do not see freshly pressed white trousers and immaculate, stainless shirts that have been packed away in a studio's wardrobe closet. Instead they should see historical characters, real people with real jobs like hunting, surveying, gardening, milking cows and hammering steel. What they should see is the mark of experience much like the marks upon the swords and shields of the early knights which displayed to other knights and onlookers the experience of the bearer. I, along with a host of my friends and acquaintances, have a good deal of experience upon our clothing. I have had shirts which fit my characters so well and which I enjoyed wearing so much that the shoulders gave out due to the constant sweat and oils soaking into the fabric and oxidizing the fibers, which led me to patch the shirts with the same or different cloth. I can usually spot a hunter who wears his frock while shooting as there are many black smudges upon the fore tails of his hunting shirt caused by wiping the frizzen or flint to remove the fowling. Furthermore, when an animal is butchered, it is hard not to get blood, tallow and other substances upon the garments. A well worn pair of shoes becomes scuffed, creased and tuned up at the toe. All these traits and characteristics show up on our garments with the same general use that our forefathers encountered.

Too, our 18th century counterparts may not have had more than one or two sets of britches at a time, and they were wearing one pair! The same goes for chemise', dresses, frock coats or waistcoats and shoes (with or without buckles). I have seen where an officer, a captain, had ordered six shirts from a seamstress, but these shirts were supposed to take him into and through the next year with one left over at the end of the year. What does all this have to do with living history, you might ask? Well the next time your vehicle is loaded to the gills with five changes of clothes for a two day/one night event, stop and think about all that excess baggage, to which, we do not give a second thought. Our cavalier attitude towards weight and bulk is due to our dependance on the internal combustion machine which does not get tired. Rather, think of a horse, or team of oxen or a canoe or York boat, all with definite limitations because if we cannot wear a second coat or set of britches then they have to be carried by someone or some animal. Oh yes! What is it that we are carrying? Ah yes. Clothing that we are supposedly going to use in our interpretation and not some faux garment that we can turn back in to the local costume shop.

The other noticeable aspect about "costume" is that the maker generally does not give a damn whether the fake garment is made out of 100% wool or 100% polyester, whether it is 100% linen or a look-a-like made from a polyester blend with not the least bit of flaxen fiber in it at all.

But to those of us who use these garments in our day-to-day lives and in our forays into the woods, or into the milk house, whether it be making a snake fence or making a meal at the hearth the seemingly insignificant detail of the actual type of fiber used allows us to step into our ancestor's shoes and know what sort of "comfort" he actually experienced not to mention discover that in many cases certain types of cloth are actually cooler and softer in the summer than our modern "casual/comfort" clothes. We can, for instance, rediscover the practicality of layering several garments upon our person, during the colder months.

So the next time you are asked about a "costume" you may have the common threads of realism and practicality woven into your various replies and thereby further educate the bearer of the question. Start by simply answering, "I am actually wearing real clothes."

7.
THE CONS OF ISOLATION

In my 23+ years of going to historical events, venues, seminars, skinner events, and juried events. I have, on occasion, come in contact with events coordinators, board members, managers and promoters and the like who do not go to any other events besides their own. Furthermore, I am shocked when attending an historic park, museum or village whether it be private, state or federal, to learn that the employees or managers do not even know of historical events within a 100 mile radius. Worse yet is, perhaps, they **do** know and make **NO effort to open up time** for themselves or their employees to attend; they are missing out on the networking which is a natural consequence of going to other venues. Isolating one's self can produce arrogance and give the impression of haughtiness and snobbery to outsiders. It creates a stagnant atmosphere. It also makes for a poor marketing plan. To some of you this may seem so obvious, like *Marketing* **101**, but I feel it simply needs to be said.

      Although I do not generally look at

attending an event as marketing, one has to remember regardless of how independent we think we are in this living history hobby, successful events are all about relationships. We meet other people at other events. We are, after all, both attending the same event. Perhaps those people know someone that we know. Now we have more than one thing in common. By getting to know as many people as you can at other historical venues you will be showing them: 1) what you do; 2) what you know; and 3) what you value. This all comes about by that most ancient and basic of means: having conversations with others. That's right, simply talking with others allows both people to get to know each other. This means we **look and listen** as well as talk.

    I am not really sure that a person can even call this approach a marketing plan, that is to say getting out and meeting others, rubbing elbows, listening to seminars (then waiting patiently to confer with the speakers) and doing for others who may one day do for you.

    I am by nature a tracker. I look at foot prints. I follow an animal based upon its behavior. We humans are no different than animals when we habitually attend a certain event. We also never stop exploring. We have a discovery sense, if you will. We feel enriched when we find another new event with good atmosphere. We leave foot prints all over the place. Our going to an event hopefully imparted a benefit to that event, and in turn we were also benefitted by meeting others in our particular living history field at that event.

Any time we can make a candid contact, there is a mutual benefit to each person much like a simple contract. Each person now knows the other in the context of the hobby, but also that one person is a blacksmith, the other a harness maker; one is a tent smith, the other a weaver; one is a tanner the other a clothier. These contacts do not stop there. We take them with us in our daily lives and we may become a reference for that person or business. When meeting people at other events, questions may come up about tents, shoes, clothes, or animal hides and we may pass on our knowledge to the inquirer of other people who are more knowledgeable about a given subject. This only comes about by getting to know the people we have met.

By doing so, the simple act of meeting another historical participant has implications many times over. Even when we are not at an event, we continue to make connections and gather information. While at home or at our regular job, whether on the phone or on the Net, we can still make contacts and pass on names of artisans, historians, and merchants to others in the field as well as those who need good information to get started. After a time, and as a result of the contact we have made, we may be asked to help with a prestigious event, an historical college project, or something similar. Best of all we will make friends whom we will cherish and with whom we will endeavor to stay in touch.

By going to other events we should have it in our minds to meet and get to know the manager, president Captain or "Booshway" as well as the "Segundo's," Scribes, etc. In the matter of a short time we will learn their aspirations (or the organization's intentions) for the coming years.

If we as managers and promoters are aware of the popularity of that particular event, not only will we enjoy attending, but we will be unlikely to schedule our own event at the same time or in conflict with it. Events that are renowned for their attention to detail and adherence to rules, will give any organizer or promoter a **benchmark** for what a well run event is and perhaps what his event could be!

We can also compare pricing of our camp with others when it comes to setting the price for the entry fees, fees for the public (if any) and other attendant costs. We should recognize when we are in step with the market place. Keeping prices in line keeps us humble. Besides it's just a camp. It's just a rendezvous. It is not the Indy-500. It is not the Super Bowl. The lesson here is to be realistic.

    I have been blessed to be a party to numerous discussions in which various managers and booshways were discussing mutual advertising for each other's event. In this approach each of the managers encourages the campers to go on to another camp (usually within a 150 mile radius) which may be the following weekend or so. The attendees and traders alike begin to create a circuit. The circuit allows the participants to attend three or more camps in a general area in a short time with a minimum of traveling. Again this may seem obvious to many, especially the traders, but there is one thing more. It is **visibility**! When you isolate you encourage INvisibility.

    Being "visible" in the general sense means staying in contact, maintaining personal contacts. More specifically, it should mean doing things like advertising in the trade journals, being willing to help with lectures, seminars or even being the speaker. Also, you leaders and scholars should consider writing short articles and news letters to let others know of the "goings on" in your neck of the woods or at your particular site. Let others know what distinguishes your site or event from all others. However, avoid pontificating...you know BS'ing people. Simply tell the participants and the public the truth as to what your event is all about and what your site has to offer. I would rather be undersold on a site and be pleasantly surprised at more amenities; than, over sold and sorely disappointed by false advertising. When people are intentionally mislead they harbor resentment which can last a long time. Resentful participants, by and large, do not continue to participate, hence the event shrinks. Event promoters who lie to public and participants gain a bad reputation which also taints the event. Granted an event does not need to be big to be good; but, if an event is losing participants faster than it is gaining them it will not be long before it folds altogether.

    All this "contact" will not be possible, though, if one does not get out. When we sit in our "little kingdoms" and do not venture out to mingle with our peers, we are depriving ourselves of mutually beneficial fellowship and a collective wisdom. You *want* to get new blood into your pool of participation. That being said, you are going to have to determine what sort of participants you are looking for and then ascertain where they hang out......... oh yea, then go there! A manager must expand his or her horizons, as the old saying goes. Remain visible. Be approachable. Be willing to go to other events and sites. Identify benchmarks to help you with patterning your event. After all, what have you got to lose, except the "cons of isolation."

CONCLUSION

GREATER HISTORICAL UNDERSTANDING

Perhaps one of the elements that would lead to a greater understanding of period camps is a basic understanding of early American history. I have received questions from any number of people who get the Revolutionary War mixed up with the Civil War. Some participants know that the French and Indian War (1756-1763) and Revolutionary War (1775-1783) both occurred in the 1700's; but, these same people also believe the terms simply refer to two parts of the same war with the same generals in the same places. Basic education in this area would go a long way to dispel this sort of confusion.

The lack of understanding seems to lead to a blending of time periods and geographical contexts. The muddling of many of these only confuses the casual participant with the result being that as long as he sees it at a rendezvous or more commonly "Ron-D-Voo" then he can mix and match anything. Worse yet, the creative mind justifies the possession of Hollywood-inspired clothing, footwear, guns, and hairstyles, because the particular item is so prevalent at camps. This concept may be referred to as the **Ron-D-Voo Syndrome.** This apt phrase was used in a pamphlet of rules issued by the Raid On Martin's Station* at the Wilderness Road State Park in the State of Virginia.

In the rules, issued by the organizers of "The Raid," it is explained that the presentation of historical figures should be based upon historical documentation referring to the particular era of (in this instance) the third Quarter of the 18th Century (1750 - 1775) and also 1776 of the common person who would have been found in Powell's Valley, Virginia. It is a tightly run event and is the type which is fosters good participation and good participants. Set in Powells Valley in the Southwestern Tip of Virginia, the camp rests below Cumberland Mountain. It is a magnificent site. As long the interpretation of the Station stays tight and organizers continue to enforce the rules, the event will continue to grow like so many others which are well maintained and have plain rules which are reasonably enforced.

Participants enjoy attending the event because it is a beautiful site and it is a tight camp. It is not a camp full of snobs. Rather, it is a camp full of people dedicated to good interpretation of the common man and woman of the 18th Century.

I must conclude that by and large, events in general do not need more rules; they do need to **enforce the rules already in place and do so consistently.** The beginner does not need to be a scholar, but watch out! Anyone who participates in historical venues can be bitten by the bug to learn more about a given era, geography, trade, or actual historical person.

The thought behind this publication is to encourage all of us to improve our events and ourselves, to give anyone of us a road map (of sorts) to organization, to ask critical questions of ourselves with the concept of How can we improve? to encourage organizers to "benchmark" by attending good, tight events, and lastly to have fun doing it.

The hobby of living history should force us all to examine our daily lives in contrast with the lives of our ancestors to allow us to enjoy the simple pleasures of a hot fire and a warm blanket on a wet, cold, rainy night. Our hobby should also allow us to appreciate the modern innovations in fields such as medicine and communication. The context of history gives us greater understanding of who we are, what we are and from whence we come. For those of you who are not purists, perhaps you will get a glimpse of what purists are looking

for in an event and why. As for you purists, perhaps this will get you thinking about other approaches or simply reassure you that you are not alone. The ideas in this publication are meant to be passed on and passed down for everyone's benefit, to provoke thought and to initiate discussion.
Thank you,
Your mst humble and ob^t servant
John W. Hayes

* Author's Note:
the name "Raid on Martin's Station" has been changed to,
    Virginia: America's First Frontier

END NOTES

1. Phone conversation between the Author and Rex Allen Norman, April 4, 2003.

2. Ibid.

3. Phone conversation between the Author and Gerry Barker, March 11, 2003.

4. Conversation between the Author and Wayne Krefting, April 1, 2006.

5. Phone converesation between Author and Mark Baker, April 13, 2003.

6. Phone conversation between the Author and H. David Wright, April 17, 2003.

7. Conversations at Mansker's Station, Tennessee, between Author and H. David Wright, May 7/8 2005.

8. Phone conversation between Author and H. David Wright, March 29, 2006.

9. Conversation bertween Author and Karl Koster at Fort Des Chartres, April 1, 2006.

10. Conversation with Mark Sage, June 24, 2006.

11. Phone conversation with John Powers of Duluth, May 24, 2006.

12. Conversation between Author and Robert Jurgena at Fort Des Chartres, April 2, 2006.

APPENDIX

I have included for the reader's review three examples of rules for events that are tightly run. All three of these events are renown and quite popular. This, however, does not ease the host's burden of enforcing compliance for ALL participants.

The first is a camp put on by the Park Rangers/interpreters at Grand Portage National Monument, a National park in Northeastern Minnesota, on the Boarder with Canada. The second is the Wilderness Road State Park in Ewing, Virginia. It is a State park and the event is organized and put on by state employed interpreters of that park. The third is private event upon State grounds which is hosted by a private organization, it is the Fort Des Chartres Colonial Trade Faire in Prairie Du Rocher, Illinois and is hosted by the group
Les Chasseurs du Datchurat.

The reader will note that the rules are clearly stated and the main theme in all three sets of rules is that the camp and people reflect an historically accurate depiction of that geographical area for the given time span. The hosts are concerned about NOT diluting the presentation of the camp. In short the participants must **stay true to their time period and geographical location.**

The reader will also note that with each event there are both unacceptable items as well as acceptable items. I have throughout this publication used both the terms Rendezvous and Ron-D-Voo. The former refers to the recreated, historic fur trade camps, the latter refers to the local club oriented events which are not necessarily based upon historical interpretation.

I wish to gratefully acknowledge the cooperation and permission of each of the three sites, Grand Portage National Monument, Minnesota; Wilderness Road State Park, Ewing Virginia, and Fort Des Chartres, Prairie du Rocher, Illinois and the Chassuers du Datcharat, for allowing me to include the respective sets of rules in this publication.

* * *

Grand Portage

The Grand Portage National Monument is part of the National Park System. Regulations and laws that govern national parks remain in effect during Rendezvous, and are frequently quite stringent. Park rangers will enforce all such regulations as appropriate.

EVENT REGULATIONS:
- Federal regulations prohibit the possession of firearms and explosives within national monuments. Therefore, bringing any firearms, including historic muskets, rifles, and/or explosives such as black powder, on site is prohibited unless written permission has been previously obtained from the Superintendent and the Historic Weapons Program Supervisor for the special event. Approved firearms, brought on-site, are subject to inspection by the park's Historic Weapons Program Supervisor. If necessary, firearms will be held and secured by the park until the event has concluded. The firearm(s) will then be returned to the owner(s). **Federal regulations specific to firearms and explosives will be strictly enforced.**

- Moderate consumption of alcoholic beverages is permitted during Rendezvous. **No alcoholic beverages are allowed outside the encampment area during publicly attended periods of Rendezvous.** Intoxication, and any improper actions as a result of being intoxicated, *will not be tolerated.* Also please be advised that the Pow Wow is an alcohol and drug free event. If you are camping with a group, please monitor alcoholic consumption so it does not become a problem. If a problem should arise, with individuals who fail to observe this policy, resulting in undue noise, disruption, or a threat to the safety and welfare of all concerned, please inform our camp bourgeois. **Do not intervene!** A park ranger will usually have better success in settling the situation and gaining compliance.

- You will be camping on historic ground. **Please do not dig fire pits.** When setting up camp, please use **only fire pits that have been provided by the National Park Service**. They will be identified and marked for you. If you are unable to locate a fire pit, please contact our camp bourgeois and he will be happy to assist you.

- Smoking is **not** permitted inside the stockade, or in any park buildings.
- Participants are **not** permitted to have pets in the historic encampment.
- A period of quiet time will be in effect between the hours of 10:00 p.m. and 7:00 a.m. each day. During this period, noise must remain at a minimum out of courtesy for fellow participants. Contact our camp bourgeois if you experience any problems with excess noise during these hours.
- Rendezvous helps us understand events at Grand Portage some 200 years ago. To keep us focused on these events, **no tent shops allowed** and blanket trading is **not acceptable** during the publicly attended periods of Rendezvous (between 9:00 AM. - 5:00PM). However, we recognize that trading among Rendezvous participants is very popular. We will permit limited trading so long as the general public is not exposed to commercialism. **Displaying sales items on blankets in front of your camp or on racks/hangers is not permitted. This regulation will be strictly enforced.**

These regulations are meant to ensure a positive experience is had by all. Thank you for your cooperation!

THE EVENT:

We seek a historically accurate depiction of Rendezvous at Grand Portage. To that end, certain equipment standards are expected of participants. We concentrate on the period 1730-1804 as well as supporting the efforts of Old Fort William. Clothing, camp equipment and materials should meet the test of being representative of the period. *We do however, want all to feel welcome. If you are lacking proper period camp equipment and materials, an appropriate campsite will be provided so that you can participate in the event.*

The primary focus of the Monument's Rendezvous is the portrayal and re-creation of such historic activities held at Grand Portage some 200 years ago. We ask that you make friendly, personal contacts with our visitors. Such contacts will help create a truly interactive event. All interpretation should stress how voyageurs, clerks, Agents, partners, and American Indians lived in the late 18th Century at Grand Portage. You can help our visitors understand what activities took place in the daily lives of these people, the problems each of them faced, and how they may have dealt with them. You can use your experiences to help bring the fur trade story of Grand Portage to life. All of our reconstructed historic structures will be accessible to historically dressed participants. *We will be in need of volunteers to cover interpretive stations at various times during the event. If you would like to volunteer your services, please sign up with our camp bourgeois. We appreciate the help.*

AVAILABLE TO OUR PARTICIPANTS: The National Park Service provides firewood, water, restrooms and trash receptacles. The Grand Portage Youth Group will deliver ice each day for a nominal fee. Park restrooms will be open 24 hours a day starting Wednesday and additional portable toilets, including a handicapped accessible toilet are located near the campsites. Sorry, there are no on-site shower facilities available. **Note: The local Trading post has moved to a new location near the lodge and casino approximately ½ mile from the encampment!**

IMPORTANT!: You will need a "ticket" for the Regale Saturday evening. There is no charge as the Regale is one way we can thank you for your participation in our event. However, you must be registered to receive a Regale "ticket." Our camp bourgeois will distribute "tickets." *On behalf of all participants, the National Park Service will be pleased to recognize the Kitchen staff for their hard work.*

GAMES & WORKSHOPS - Some historic games and contests are open only to costumed participants. These events will be marked with a (**) next to the event listed in the event schedule. A reminder: workshops on Friday and Saturday are also open to the public, and will have a limited number of openings, so participation is on a first-come-first-served basis. There may also be fees for supplies and materials. **Please sign up for workshops at the information tent by the main gate.** Parents may sign only their own children up for workshops. The children need not be present, but we ask that parents respect the posted age limit for our workshops. Given the limited amount of space in most workshops, (Special kid's workshops excepted) we ask that only one member from each family sign up for any given workshop, then share the skills with their family members back in camp. Doing so gives the most people the chance to learn a new skill. However, participants can sign up for more than one workshop during our event so long as they are the only member of their immediate family in any particular workshop. There will be no workshops or games scheduled during the Pow-Wow Grand Entry. We encourage all that are interested to enjoy the Grand Entry and other Pow-Wow events.

We welcome your comments and suggestions regarding Rendezvous. Comment forms are available at the tent next to the main gate.

ON COMING AND GOING:
You must be registered to participate in the event. Please see our camp bourgeois to register and be assigned a campsite. The following schedule applies for set-up and takedown.
    Wednesday...[date]-Set Up Begins after 5:00PM (Vehicles Allowed)
    Thursday.......[date]-Set Up All Day (Vehicles Allowed)
    Friday...........[date]-Set Up (No Vehicles Allowed between 9:00AM & 5:00PM)
    Saturday........[date]-(No Vehicles Allowed)
    Sunday..........[date]-Takedown (No Vehicles Allowed before 3:00PM*)*
Our camp bourgeois will be on-site and available to assist you during the entire Rendezvous event. In addition to helping you get settled, our bourgeois will have your Regale "tickets" and additional event information.

CAMP EQUIPMENT:
- The use of a canvas wedge tent. Lean-to, or **small** wall tent is encouraged. **Baker tents, tipis and 1-poles are not allowed. Supply tents are discouraged. No tent can be larger than 10' x 15' in size. No stove pipes please!**
- Modern equipment such as coolers, sleeping bags, cameras, and plastics must be kept covered or stored out of sight.
- For safety, please keep trade axes and knives in appropriate sheaths.
- Wood, tin, ceramic, copper, brass and iron are all acceptable. cookware. No modern enamelware or aluminum please.

• Clay pipes and chewing tobacco are acceptable, but no cigarettes please.
• **All historic flags and banners displayed on canoes or within a camp should be representative of the time period interpreted during Rendezvous. You will be asked to remove any flags or banners that are not appropriate for our event.**

<u>FUR TRADE FASHIONS</u>:
Typical men's clothing may have included:
• Long-sleeved shirts made from a natural fabric such as linen, cotton, or wool. Please avoid polyester or non-period prints.
• Drop front or French fly breeches or pants. Leggings and breech clouts.
• A blanket coat or capote.
• a woven sash and leg ties.
• Head wear such as knit-style caps or tuques. Beaver, rabbit, or wool felt hats. Scarves of a period fabric.
• Moccasins or cobbled shoes of a period appropriate design.
• **Ren-Fair and "Pirate" style clothing is not appropriate to our event.**

Typical Women's clothing may have included:
• Strap dresses, leggings, and sleeves made from a natural fabric such as linen, cotton, or wool. Please avoid polyester or non-period prints. Western style buckskin dresses are discouraged.
• Skirts, chemises, short-gowns and Empire dresses.
• Moccasins of a period appropriate design.
• A woven sash.
• shawls and wool blankets for outerwear.
• scarves, beads, and trade silver representative of the period.

JUST GETTING STARTED? If you have recently become interested in the fur trade era and would like to have more help in putting you historic clothing and equipment together, give us a call! We are happy to put you in touch with folks who can help and have historic clothing information available. Contact Grand Portage Monument, P.O. Box 668, Grand Marais, MN 55604. Phone TTY:(218) 387-2788.

Wilderness Road State Park

MANDATORY GUIDELINES

1. Please remain in period clothing at all times. Vehicles are not permitted in the program area after 8:00AM Friday. Your appearance camp, accoutrements, food, etc, will be reviewed by park interpretive staff for authenticity.

2. All items used or sold at the Raid at Martins Station will be authentic to 1750 - 1776. This includes clothing, furnishings, guns, knives, shoes, hats, baggage, eating utensils, cooking utensils, trunks, etc. No Western or Plains Indian articles should be used or sold. The following items may not be sold: *Chinese bamboo flutes *hatchets, *popguns, *Archaeological artifacts, *Items representing post 1776, *Holiday items *Mass-produced items (T-shirts, etc.) Skins of domestic animals *Souvenir-type items *Photographs *pictures, or *stationary *cds and tapes may be sold but must remain hidden at all times.

3. Only 18th Century style eye-wear, facsimiles or contact lenses will be allowed. Modern eye-wear is not acceptable.

4. Men's clothing and appearance includes typical 18th Century colonial apparel. The following items are not allowed: calico shirts, long fringed buckskins, "Mountain man" clothing, western clothing, and capotes. Facial hair is acceptable, but please, no sideburns or goatees.

5. Women's clothing and appearance includes typical 18th Century colonial apparel. Simple gowns, petticoats, shifts, short gowns or bed jackets. Jewelry should be appropriate to the 18th Century only.

6. Footwear allowed includes 18th Century style shoes and moccasins. Modern footwear, modern moccasins, slippers, Mary Jane's or Chinese slippers are not acceptable.

7. Shelters accepted include simple lean-to's/diamond flys, marquees, wedge or wall tents. Civil War tent, Teepees, Bakers, Walans, Center

poles or nylon tents will not be allowed.

8. Coolers are allowed in the tent area, but coolers and other non-period items are to be left outside the program area (the area around the Fort, surrounded by split rail fence). The parking area is a short distance from the program area so keep your perishable foods in this location.

9. No food or drink is to be served unless you have an 18th Century period cup, mug, or plate, etc.

10. **Alcoholic beverages are not permitted by order of Virginia State Park regulations.**

11. No cigarettes, brown cigar-like cigarettes, or cigars are allowed at any time while you are in period clothing. This includes the parking area, rest rooms, etc. Only 18th Century period pipes are permitted.

12. Pets are allowed, however, all dogs MUST be restrained by a leash not exceeding 6ft in length and under the owner's control at all times, this is Virginia State law. Breeds should be appropriate to your persona and on an appropriate 18th Century leash at all times. Anyone wanting to bring horses to this event **MUST** contact Park Staff two weeks prior to the event. There are special equine regulations that must be followed.

13. Minor children are the sole responsibility of their parents. Children will not be allowed to run around unattended, or play around fires, tools, or animals at any time. Young children need to be supervised by parents at all times.

14. No cameras are to be used while you are attired in period clothing.

15. No firearms can be carried outside of the historic area (i.e. trails, parking lots, etc.) Firearms are allowed in period camps only. Firearms cannot be carried by minors at any time. To insure the safety of visitors, participants and staff, all firearms will be inspected each morning. Only staff, and selected volunteers can demonstrate a

firearm. A staff member must be notified before the demonstration of any firearm. Only adults will handle edged weapons, or tools.

16. Tables must be correct to 18th Century or skirted to the ground. No modern staples may be used to secure the covering.

Fort Des Chartres Colonial Trade Faire and Rifle & Musket Frolic

THIS EVENT IS BEING PUT ON FOR REENACTORS WHO DEMAND THE HIGHEST LEVEL OF AUTHENTICITY ACHIEVABLE. WE UNDERSTAND THESE REGULATIONS MAY BE HARD FOR SOME TO ABIDE BY. IF YOU CAN'T ADHERE TO THE RULES, PLEASE DO NOT BOTHER APPLYING.

Mandatory Rules -

1. Your appearance, camp, accoutrements, goods, etc. will be inspected for authenticity by the Chasseurs du Datchurat and/or their agents. If you have questionable items, please be prepared to provide documentation. The burden of proof shall be on the bearer of disputed items.

2. While on the Fort grounds, **YOU ARE IN THE 18TH CENTURY!** All items are required to reflect this philosophy. Participants must remain in period clothing at all times.

3. **ABSOLUTELY NO PLASTIC IS ALLOWED!** This means **NO PLASTIC GROUND TARPS, WATER JUGS, TABLES, PACKAGING...** Bottom line - if it's not right, don't bring it!

4. All items used or sold at the Faire will be authentic to the 1750 - 1790 time period. This includes clothing, furnishing, guns, knives,

shoes, hats, baggage, cooking and eating utensils, trunks, etc. All items will be germane to the Illinois country of 1750 - 1790. No bamboo flutes or toy weapons are to be sold

5. **MODERN EYE WEAR IS UNACCEPTABLE, UNACCEPTABLE, UNACCEPTABLE, UNACCEPTABLE,** Only 18th Century eye-wear, facsimiles, or contact lenses are acceptable.

6. Men's clothing must be typical 18th Century Colonial dress. The following are examples of **UNACCEPTABLE** garments: calico shirts, long fringed buckskins. "Mountain Man" And Plains Indian clothing, Cowboy hats, and Rocky Mountain style Capotes. Modern Scottish Highland Dress and 20th Century Native American Ceremonial Dress will not be allowed.

7. Women's Clothing must be typical 18th Century Colonial dress; simple petticoats, shifts, short gowns. Bed jackets. White or off white caps should be worn by ladies 15 years of age or older - documentation is available for women in the Illinois country wearing their hair down without caps, however this practice considered unbecoming . Jewelry should be appropriate to the 18th Century. 18th Century Great Lakes and Ohio Valley Indian Dress is appropriate

The following are **UNACCEPTABLE**: Plains two and three hide dresses, makeup, calico prints, "prairie dresses" and "prairie sunbonnets."

8. Footwear allowed includes 18th Century style shoes, boots, and moccasins ONLY!

The following are **UNACCEPTABLE**: Dyer and Poppen Moccasins, engineer boots, cowboy boots slippers, Victorian era lace up boots, and Chinese slippers.

9. Shelters accepted include simple lean-tos, diamond shelters, marquee, wedge, or wall tents.

The following will NOT be accepted: Tipi's, Whelan Lean-tos, Baker tents, and One-pole tents.

10. All coolers and other non-period items should remain in your vehicle. The parking area is a short distance from the grounds, so keep perishable foods in your car.

11. No food or drink is to be consumed unless it is in a proper 18th Century vessel.

12. **NO CIGARETTES, OR BROWN CIGAR-LIKE CIGARETTES ARE ALLOWED ON THE GROUNDS AT ANY TIME.** Only 18th Century period style pipes are permitted.

13. Minor children are the sole responsibility of their parents.
14. **Sorry, but unfortunately NO PETS are allowed on the Fort grounds. This is a mandate that is being enforced by the state. The event hosts or the Fort management have no say in this matter.**
15. No cameras are to be used while attired in period clothing.
16. Guns shall be loaded only on the shooting range. **FIRING OF BLANK ROUNDS IS PROHIBITED.**

General Rules -

A. Vehicles are not permitted on the grounds between 8:00 am Saturday and 3:00 pm Sunday. Participants should be prepared to pack in or pack out in the event of wet grounds.

B. Once setting up camp is complete, appropriate clothing must be worn until camp is taken down.

C. All musical instruments must be appropriate to the 18th Century. Songs, whether bawdy or not, must be appropriate to the 18th Century (no bluegrass, cowboy, or country and western music.)

D. **First person Interpretation is encouraged**.

E. Both the Musket and Rifle frolics are blanket shoots, requiring each participant to provide a prize of a minimum $20 value.

**THERE WILL BE NO EXCEPTIONS TO THE RULES!
DO NOT ASK FOR ANY TO BE GIVEN.**

NOTES